JOHN ELWAY
and the
Denver Broncos

SUPER BOWL XXXIII

by Michael Sandler

Consultant: Norries Wilson
Head Football Coach
Columbia University

BEARPORT
PUBLISHING

New York, New York

Credits

Cover and Title Page, © Al Bello/Getty Images; 4, © Doug Collier/AFP/Getty Images; 5, © Tom Hauck/Getty Images; 6, © Courtesy Granada Hills Charter High School; 7, © Courtesy Granada Hills Charter High School; 8, © Bettmann/Corbis; 10, © AP Images/Wilfredo Lee; 11, © George Rose/Getty Images; 12, © NFL/WireImage.com; 13, © Richard Mackson/Sports Illustrated; 14, © REUTERS; 15, © Al Messerschmidt/WireImage.com; 16, © Al Tielemans/Sports Illustrated; 17, © Walter Looss Jr./Sports Illustrated; 18, © Brian Bahr/Allsport/Getty Images; 19, © REUTERS/Pierre Ducharme; 20, © AP Images/Doug Mills; 21, © Tim Clary/AFP/Getty Images; 22L, © AP Images/Denis Poroy; 22R, © AP Images/John Froschauer; 22 Background, © AP Images/Wilfredo Lee.

Publisher: Kenn Goin
Senior Editor: Lisa Wiseman
Creative Director: Spencer Brinker
Design: Deborah Kaiser
Photo Researcher: Jennifer Bright

Library of Congress Cataloging-in-Publication Data

Sandler, Michael.
 John Elway and the Denver Broncos : Super Bowl XXXIII / by Michael Sandler.
    p. cm. — (Super Bowl superstars)
 Includes bibliographical references and index.
 ISBN-13: 978-1-59716-536-5 (library binding)
 ISBN-10: 1-59716-536-0 (library binding)
1. Elway, John, 1960– Juvenile literature. 2. Football players—United States—Biography—Juvenile literature. 3. Denver Broncos (Football team)— Juvenile literature. 4. Super Bowl (33rd : 1999 : Miami, Fla.)—Juvenile literature. I. Title.

 GV939.E48S26 2008
 796.332092—dc22
 (B)

2007010312

For more information, write to Bearport Publishing Company, Inc., 101 Fifth Avenue, Suite 6R, New York, New York 10003. Printed in the United States of America.

10 9 8 7 6 5 4 3

★ Contents ★

One Last Game

For over 15 years, quarterback John Elway had been the Denver Broncos' biggest star. Since the 1980s, he had thrilled fans with his dazzling passing and game-winning **drives**.

Football, however, had worn down John's 38-year-old body. He ached after every throw. In his heart, John knew that Super Bowl XXXIII (33) would be his last game. He wanted to walk away a champion. To do so, he would need to lead Denver to a victory.

Fans show their support for John Elway.

John before Super Bowl
XXXIII (33) in 1999

BRONCOS

John was one of only
two NFL quarterbacks to
throw for over 50,000 yards
(45,720 m) in his career.

Expecting Success

John's NFL success was no surprise. People always knew he'd be a star. The only question was in which sport. As a teenager, he was fantastic in both football and baseball.

In high school, John's strong and **accurate** passing made him the country's most highly **recruited** football player. He was also **drafted** by baseball's Kansas City Royals. However, John wasn't ready to give up either sport yet. So he decided to go to Stanford University and play both.

John playing baseball for Granada Hills High School in California

John played quarterback for his high school team.

John got **scholarship** offers from over 50 colleges.

Stanford Star

In four years at Stanford, John threw for almost 10,000 yards (9,144 m). He could also run the ball, making him an even more dangerous player.

In the 1983 National Football League (NFL) draft, the Baltimore Colts chose him with the very first pick. Soon afterward, Baltimore **traded** him to the Denver Broncos. Denver fans couldn't believe their luck.

John (#7) on the field with his Stanford Cardinal teammates

In 1982, John threw more touchdown passes than any other college quarterback.

BRONCOS
QB
topps

John's rookie NFL football card

Super Bowl Bound

John didn't disappoint the fans. He became known as a **clutch** passer, winning games on the final drive.

In his second year in the NFL, he helped Denver to a 13-3 record. Then in 1987, he took the team into Super Bowl XXI (21).

John threw well, but it wasn't enough for Denver. The New York Giants **overwhelmed** the Broncos' **defense** in an easy 39-20 victory.

John's (#7) 98-yard (90-m) drive against the Cleveland Browns helped put Denver in Super Bowl XXI (21).

John led the Broncos in rushing and threw for over 300 yards (274 m) in Super Bowl XXI (21).

Winless

Despite the Super Bowl loss, Broncos fans were hopeful. John was just getting better and better. Sooner or later he would lead Denver to a title.

Somehow, however, it didn't happen. Denver returned to the Super Bowl two more times, in 1988 and 1990. They lost both games, first to the Washington Redskins and then to the San Francisco 49ers.

The Washington Redskins celebrate their Super Bowl win in 1988.

In Super Bowl XXIV (24), the 49ers beat the Broncos, 55-10.

Taking the Blame

The Super Bowl losses weren't just John's fault. Football is a team sport. In each of the three games, the other teams were clearly better.

Still, when a football team loses, a quarterback gets the blame. People blamed John. Only a Super Bowl victory would change their minds.

A reporter once asked John if he would trade all his passing records for a Super Bowl win. "In a heartbeat," John replied.

Elway (#7) led Denver to the playoffs five times in the 1990s.

John talks
with reporters.

Only two other
teams have lost as many
Super Bowls as Denver—
the Buffalo Bills and the
Minnesota Vikings.

Sweet Success

In 1998, Denver returned to the Super Bowl. Most people picked their **opponent**, the **NFC**'s Green Bay Packers, to win the game.

NFC teams had won 13 straight Super Bowls. Denver was an **AFC** team, so people expected them to lose. They also remembered the Broncos' recent Super Bowl failures.

This time Denver didn't disappoint their fans. The Broncos beat Green Bay, 31-24. At last, John was a Super Bowl champion!

Terrell Davis (#30) scores one of his three touchdowns for Denver.

Denver's victory in Super Bowl XXXII (32) was the team's first in five Super Bowl appearances.

Sweet Redemption

best Super Bowl ever, John Elway finally finishes on top

Facing the Falcons

Afterward, many people thought John would **retire**. His body was bruised and battered from hundreds of NFL games.

To John, however, victory was sweet. He wanted to experience it again. He returned the next season and led the Broncos into Super Bowl XXXIII (33).

Denver's opponent, the Atlanta Falcons, scored first. However, John came right back. At halftime, Denver led, 17-6.

At 38 years old, John was the oldest quarterback ever to start in a Super Bowl.

Rod Smith (#80) runs for an 80-yard (73-m) touchdown for the Broncos.

One Final Victory

In the second half, John kept up his excellent passing. He also showed off his running skills. In the fourth quarter, he carried the ball for a touchdown.

Whenever Atlanta attacked, the Broncos' defense made big plays. Twice **cornerback** Darrien Gordon **intercepted** passes to stop Atlanta.

When the game was over, Denver had a second straight Super Bowl victory. John, voted the game's **MVP**, was a Super Bowl champion again!

John (#7) makes a touchdown.

John retired after
Super Bowl XXXIII (33).

★ Key Players ★

There were other key players on the Denver Broncos who helped win Super Bowl XXXIII (33). Here are two of them.

★ Darrien Gordon #21

Position: Cornerback

Born: 11/14/1970 in Shawnee, Oklahoma

Height: 5' 11" (1.8 m)

Weight: 190 pounds (86 kg)

Key Plays: Intercepted two passes from the Falcons' quarterback Chris Chandler

★ Rod Smith #80

Position: Wide Receiver

Born: 5/15/1970 in Texarkana, Arkansas

Height: 6' 0" (1.83 m)

Weight: 200 pounds (91 kg)

Key Plays: Caught 5 passes for 152 yards (139 m) and a touchdown

accurate (AK-yuh-ruht)
exact; free from mistakes

AFC (AY-EFF-SEE)
American Football Conference; one of the two conferences in the NFL

clutch (KLUHCH)
able to stay calm and do well in difficult situations

cornerback (KOR-nur-bak)
a player on defense who usually covers the other team's receivers

defense (DEE-fenss)
players who have the job of stopping the other team from scoring

drafted (DRAFT-id)
picked after college to play for an NFL team

drives (DRIVEZ)
a series of plays that begin when a team gets the ball; the plays end when the team either scores or gives up the ball to the other team

intercepted (*in*-tur-SEPT-id)
caught a pass meant for a player on the other team

MVP (EM-VEE-PEE)
the most valuable player in a game or season

NFC (EN-EFF-SEE)
National Football Conference; one of the two conferences in the NFL

opponent (uh-POH-nuhnt)
a team that another team plays against in a sporting event

overwhelmed (*oh*-vur-WELMD)
completely outplayed, crushed

recruited (ri-KROOT-id)
sought after, asked to join

retire (ri-TIE-ur)
to end one's career

scholarship (SKOL-ur-ship)
an award that pays for a person to go to college

traded (TRADE-id)
exchanged one player for a player on another team

Bibliography

Sports Illustrated. *John Elway: The Drive of a Champion.* New York: Simon & Schuster (1998).

The New York Times

www.denverbroncos.com

Read More

LeBoutillier, Nate. *Denver Broncos: Super Bowl Champions.* Mankato, MN: Creative Education (2005).

Schmalzbauer, Adam. *The History of the Denver Broncos.* Mankato, MN: Creative Education (2004).

Walters, John. *AFC West: American Football Conference West.* Mankato, MN: Child's World (2005).

Learn More Online

To learn more about John Elway, the Denver Broncos, and the Super Bowl, visit **www.bearportpublishing.com/SuperBowlSuperstars**

Index